ISBN 0 573 12154 0

Please see page iv for further copyright information

LITTLEBRO MORNING
AND BIGSIS AFTERNOON

First performed by the Kirkintilloch Players at the Village
Theatre, East Kilbride, on 13th Febuary 1998, with the following
cast:

Young Dunkie	Gavin M. Paterson
Young Lottie	Greer McGroarty
Fred	Gavin Paterson
Christine	Julie Logan
Dunkie	Paul Docherty
Lottie	Aine Rice
Dad	Mike Tibbetts
Mrs Reid	Myra Scott
Clerk	Val Gumley
Mr Grant(Bank Manager)	David Mitchell

Directed by Pam Tibbetts

This production reached the national final of the Scottish
Community Drama Association Festival in 1998

COPYRIGHT INFORMATION
(See also page ii)

CHARACTERS

Lottie, *a schoolgirl; twelve years old*
Dunkie, *Lottie's brother; seven years old*
Fred, *a social worker*
Christine, *a social worker*
Dad, *Lottie's and Dunkie's father*
Mrs Reid, *Lottie's home economics teacher*
Mr Grant, *a bank manager*
Clerk, *in Mr Grant's bank*

The action of the play takes place between Lottie's and Dunkie's suburban house, their local Social Services department, a room in Lottie's school and the manager's office in a local bank
Time — Interweaving between the present and the past

AUTHOR'S NOTE

This play reflects grown-ups' difficulty in sharing a child's view of reality. It is important, therefore, that the children and their motivations are portrayed with clarity and depth but without any mawkishness.

I believe that this can be achieved in two quite different ways.

Companies with young actors strong enough to sustain lead roles may cast Lottie and Dunkie with children of the right age. In this case the performances may well benefit from the youngsters' instinctive reaction to their situation and it is probable that young performers will have the greatest emotional impact on audiences.

Alternatively, adult actors may play the children. It may bring an extra dimension to their portrayal, having adult actors inhabit the minds and the world of the children. But there should be no doubt that they are real children as opposed to adults remembering or role-playing. If adult actors are used it is suggested that children play Lottie and Dunkie in the non-speaking scenes at the opening and closing of the play. This script includes directions to accommodate this.

Mike Tibbetts

For Kirsty and Jamie

and with thanks to

Les Price

for professional advice

Also by Mike Tibbetts
published by Samuel French

One Act Play
Bottles With Baskets On

LITTLEBRO MORNING
AND BIGSIS AFTERNOON

Dunkie's bedroom. This is a seven-year-old boy's bedroom, decorated and equipped as you'd find in a comfortably-off home. The room is cluttered with toys, books and things. There is a bed, perhaps a bunk bed, with a mound of colourful bedding that covers Dunkie sleeping, and a chair with an incongruous pile of neatly folded clothes

The stage is in semi-darkness

Lottie, a young girl aged twelve, enters and comes to the front of the stage, rubbing her eyes. She is frowzy from just waking up and is wearing a long tee-shirt as a nightdress. She carries her diary, a cheap exercise book, clasped to her breast. The book has a ballpoint pen clipped to its cover and an official-looking brown window envelope sticking out from the pages. She mimes opening curtains or lifting a blind

The bedroom floods with morning sunlight

Lottie pauses, yawning

Dunkie, a little boy aged seven wearing brightly-coloured pyjamas, turns over in his sleep and the mound of bedclothes on the bunk stirs. His limbs scatter in an abandoned sprawl and one arm is flung out of the bed at an odd angle. But he remains deeply asleep

Lottie turns towards the bed at this movement. She sees Dunkie's arm, lays down her diary, approaches the bed and takes his hand gently in hers. She examines it, as if it were some precious object. Then she presses it tenderly against her cheek and closes her eyes

Cross-fade to Christine and Fred

Christine and Fred are seated around an office desk, strewn with official-looking files and a jumble of paper. They are social workers. Christine is younger than Fred. They are both dressed casually

Christine and Fred are reading papers in manilla files. His file is thick and dog-eared and her file is new and containing only a few papers. It is well through a tiring day

Christine   You got kids, Fred?

Fred   (*still absorbed in his reading*) Used to.

Christine (*with professional understanding*) Live with their mother, do they?

Fred   No. (*He looks up*) With their girlfriends. You?

Christine   No. (*She puts down her file*) You'd think it would be required. I mean, here I am, sorting out dysfunctional kids and inadequate parents. You think they'd expect me to have some practical experience. Maybe not, though. Maybe we're like priests ——

Fred   (*without much force*) Bloody hell! (*He goes back to reading his file*)

Christine   What I mean is, maybe not being a parent yourself lets you be more objective. You know, see things from the kids' point of view a bit.

Fred   (*putting down his file*) Christine, I was never the world's greatest parent. But one thing I did learn is that adults can never really see things from a kid's point of view.

Cross-fade back to Dunkie's bedroom

The scene is exactly as we left it: Lottie still holds Dunkie's hand against her cheek. If it is intended that Lottie and Dunkie are to be played by adults, this is where the change-over becomes apparent. The adults' appearances must be similar to the children; mirroring Lottie's pose and Dunkie's sprawl across the bed

Lottie sighs, releases the boy's hand and shakes his arm

Lottie C'mon, Dunkie.

Dunkie murmurs from the bed and burrows deeper into the mound of bedclothes

Time to wake up!

Lottie moves away from the bed and picks up her diary. She squats on the floor and takes the envelope, which is already torn open, from between the book's pages. She takes out a folded sheet of paper from inside and starts to read it. This is not the first time she has read it. It seems unwelcome. Her lips tighten and she frowns as she scans the page. Lottie sighs, unclips the pen from the cover of her diary and starts to make a note in the book

Dunkie's tousled head pops out of the bedclothes. He rubs his eyes and looks around. Half-asleep, he smiles at the bright sunlight

Lottie is still absorbed in her writing

Dunkie My bedroom's full of morning!
Lottie Yes.
Dunkie (*brighter*) Is it my *special* morning?

Lottie is caught, in some way, by Dunkie's last question. She pauses. Her hand, carrying the pen, is suspended in mid-air for a moment. With effort, she tries to keep her tone light as she speaks to Dunkie

Lottie Yes. It's your special morning.

Dunkie leaps up to a kneeling position in his bed, as if he is on springs

Dunkie Great! I can really do anything I want for a whole morning?

Lottie That's what we agreed. (*She packs up her diary and rises to rest her arms on the rail of the bed*) What do you want to do?

Dunkie (*frowning*) I wish we could watch television.

Lottie Well, we can't. You know that.

Dunkie Why did we have to sell the television, Lottie?

Lottie To buy your shoes.

Dunkie I'd rather have television than shoes.

Lottie (*firmly*) You need decent shoes.

Dunkie (*taking a different tack*) I want Choccos, then. Choccos for breakfast.

Lottie All right.

Dunkie With raisins—and maple syrup—— (*He watches Lottie carefully*)

Lottie frowns but nods

—and chocolate sauce?

Lottie Yuk!

Dunkie OK. No chocolate sauce. But in bed.

Lottie Oh, no, Dunkie.

Dunkie Please, *Lottie.*

Lottie You'll mess up the bedclothes —(*pause*) well, I suppose that doesn't matter now. (*Something clouds her face for an instant. She forces herself to be bright again*) I'll go and get it. You get dressed.

She picks up the chair, with the pile of clothes, and brings it nearer to the bed

I'll race you. See if you can get dressed before I make the breakfast. (*She turns to exit*)

Dunkie (*picking up a garment from the chair*) These are school clothes.

Lottie I know.

Dunkie You said it wasn't school today.

Lottie It isn't. I just want you smart, that's all.

Dunkie Why?

Lottie Got to be smart for your special morning.

Lottie exits

Dunkie struggles to get dressed on his own

Cross-fade to Christine and Fred

Fred Is that the new case?
Christine Yes. The two kids.
Fred Mind if I have a look?

Christine hands him the file

Fred scans the first paper and then leafs through the others

Fred Do we know what happened to the mother?
Christine Car accident. That big pile-up on the by-pass.
Fred That's a while ago.
Christine Nearly two years. I remember it. Terrible thing. They'd
  only moved here a few weeks before.
Fred Where from?
Christine Don't know, yet.
Fred So what about the father?
Christine Don't know that, either. We've got the police on to it.
  There's nothing on file, apparently. We just don't have any
  information.
Fred Look, Christine, somebody must know something about this
  family.
Christine (*looking at him balefully*) Says who? (*She picks up
  Lottie's diary from the desk. The envelope isn't in it*) Have you
  seen this?
Fred What is it?
Christine Her diary.
Fred What, the mother's?
Christine No. Hers. (*Leafing through the pages of the diary*) She
  wrote it all down. Every detail. Day after day for four months.
  Right up until today.
Fred (*reaching over*) Can I have a look?

Christine passes him the diary

Fred leafs through Lottie's diary. He pauses to take more notice of a page towards the back

Here it is. "May the tenth. Our Special Day". (*He looks enquiringly at Christine*)
Christine Oh, just wait till you read it.

Cross-fade to Dunkie's bedroom

Lottie brings in a tray. This bears a colourful plastic bowl filled with cereal, a matching cup of juice and a teacup with a single small flower in it. Lottie is wearing her school clothes

Dunkie springs to attention with his clothes in whatever state he has reached

Dunkie I win!
Lottie (*looking at the dishevelled state of him*) Yeah, right.
Dunkie I do! I'm dressed!
Lottie Let me just finish you off. (*She puts the tray down and straightens up his clothing*)

Dunkie notices the flower

Dunkie What's the flower for?
Lottie For you.
Dunkie Why?
Lottie For your special morning.
Dunkie But what's it for?
Lottie To make things special. Daddy used to bring Mummy flowers.
Dunkie (*quietly*) I don't remember Mummy.
Lottie (*pauses, saddened by this*) I know.
Dunkie I'm sorry I forgot.
Lottie It's all right. You were only four.

Dunkie Why did Daddy bring Mummy flowers?
Lottie To tell her he loved her. That's what flowers are for.

Dunkie flings his arms round Lottie

Dunkie I love you, BigSis!
Lottie (*with distance in her eyes*) And I love you, LittleBro.
Dunkie (*skipping to his bunk*) Breakfast in bed!
Lottie Oh, Dunkie, I don't want you all messed up.
Dunkie Please, Lottie. You promised. For my special morning.
Lottie I didn't promise. Anyway, you've got your smart clothes on
    now.
Dunkie Awww!
Lottie Look, I tell you what. Even better than breakfast in bed, how
    about a picnic breakfast? Right here. I'll put it all out on the floor
    and you can have it as a picnic in here.
Dunkie (*unconvinced*) That's not a picnic. Picnics are outside.
Lottie Come on, Dunkie. I'll read you a story while you eat your
    picnic.
Dunkie OK. (*He sits down on the floor and starts to eat from the
    bowl of cereal*)
Lottie I'll get the book.

Lottie exits

Cross-fade to Christine and Fred

Fred looks up from reading Lottie's diary

Christine See what I mean?
Fred (*shrugging*) She made breakfast for her little brother. So
    what?
Christine Not just breakfast — she thought up this idea of a whole
    special morning for him.
Fred Why?
Christine Because it was the last one. Because she knew that in the
    afternoon ... (*She breaks off*) Don't you see?
Fred See what?

Christine You haven't got an ounce of sentiment, have you?

Fred No. Not when I'm doing my job. And neither should you.

Christine Oh, come on, Fred. Isn't that what social work is supposed to be all about— looking at the human side of things?

Fred That's sensitivity, not sentimentality. When you get sentimental ——

Christine You think I'm getting sentimental?

Fred I don't know. You started this. But for what it's worth, I think getting sentimental about a case means you start romanticising the situation, making it up for yourself, the way you would like it to be. And then you lose sight of the way things really are.

Christine Hey, I don't have to make anything up. (*She grabs the diary*) It's all here. Look. (*She thrusts the book at Fred*)

Cross-fade to Dad

Dad, early middle-aged, is sitting in an armchair. He is dressed in a suit and tie. The suit looks rumpled and seedy. There is a briefcase beside the armchair. It is placed as if he has come in from work. Holding a TV remote control, Dad is rhythmically, almost manically, zapping through channels on the television. He looks as though he is searching desperately for something but he remains uninterested as the programmes cycle round and round.

The TV may be suggested by a flashing light on his face, but we don't hear anything

Lottie enters

Lottie is dressed in her school clothes and is holding a newspaper. She is tentative, nervous of her father's mood

Lottie Dad?

Dad gives no response

I've done my homework. (*Pause*) I couldn't understand number four. It's a graph and I can't do them.

Dad still gives no response

Lottie continues, as if talking to herself

It's all right. I'll ask somebody at school tomorrow. (*Pause*) You're supposed to sign my homework, but I've signed it for you. It's all right, I've done it all properly — as properly as I can, anyway. Oh, by the way. Don't worry about parents' night next week. I told Mrs Reid that you were away on business. She understood— I think.

Lottie shifts her feet uncomfortably, preparing to raise a difficult subject

Dad?

Dad still doesn't answer

Lottie touches his arm

Dad reacts with a startled jerk

Dad (*angrily*) What?
Lottie (*through gritted teeth*) I need some money, Dad.
Dad What do you need money for?
Lottie Not for me. The window cleaner. We owe him three months and he says he won't come again if we don't pay him.

Dad ignores her

Dad, we've got to pay the bills.
Dad Oh, Lottie, please! I've — just come in. Ask me later.
Lottie OK. (*A brief pause*) Dad? When are you going to stop being so sad?
Dad You're just a kid. What do you know about being sad?
Lottie She was my mum.
Dad Yes, but she was my wife, Lottie. You don't know what that means. I loved her. Long before you came along. Really loved her. I — just lived for her.

Lottie Can't you live for me and Dunkie now, Dad?

Dad I try. (*Suddenly looking at her*) You know that, don't you, Lottie? I do try.

Lottie (*without much conviction*) Yes, Dad.

Dad And we're OK aren't we? I know that things have been difficult, but we're managing?

Lottie Yes.

Dad You can cope, can't you?

Lottie Yes, Dad. I can cope.

Dad (*while hunting for his wallet*) The window cleaner you said. How much is it?

Lottie Fifteen pounds.

Dad Fifteen pounds?

Lottie I told you. It's three months.

Dad I haven't got that much on me. Look ... (*He takes out a bank debit card and hands it to Lottie*) you can get it out of the bank machine. You know how to use one, don't you?

Lottie Yes, but I need the number.

Dad Eight, four, six, three. Can you remember that?

Lottie Yes.

Dad You're a good girl.

Lottie Will you go to bed tonight, Dad?

Dad What for? I haven't slept properly for months. Not since ...

Lottie You need sleep. You'll be too tired to do your work.

Dad (*with a snort*) Work!

Lottie You have to work, Dad. It's important.

Dad Oh, Lottie, you don't understand. Leave me alone!

Lottie Yes, Dad. (*She turns away*)

Cross-fade to Christine and Fred

Fred Do we know what the father did for a living?

Christine Self-employed, as far as we can tell. Consultant or something. Don't know more than that.

Fred Shouldn't be too hard for the police to track him down. He must have customers, business contacts and so on. They'll find him.

Christine If he wants to be found.

Fred What do you mean?

Christine Well, isn't it right that even if they find him, the police can't tell us where he is unless he gives them permission?

Fred Yes, but why wouldn't he want to be back with his kids?

Christine Why would he walk out on them?

Fred He's depressed. He needs a bit of help, that's all.

Christine If he's that depressed, isn't there a chance he might have … you know?

Fred It's possible, but let's think positive for now. Let's just find dad, get them together again as a family and back them up with a bit of support. And the sooner the better. Do you think there might be a clue in there — (*he nods towards the diary*) you know — where he might have gone?

Christine Maybe. You wouldn't believe what's in here. Every detail.

Cross-fade to Dunkie's bedroom

Lottie is writing in her diary

Dunkie (*off*) Lottie! Where are you?

Lottie I'm up here.

Dunkie enters, dragging his school bag

Dunkie Where's Dad?

Lottie He's not here.

Dunkie Awww! Isn't he back *yet*?

Lottie No.

Dunkie Where is he?

Lottie I told you. He's away at a conference.

Dunkie What's a confluence?

Lottie Not a confluence. A conference.

Dunkie How long does a — confence —go on?

Lottie A long time. Days sometimes. Done your homework?

Dunkie Haven't got any.

Lottie Don't believe you.
Dunkie It's true!
Lottie Truly true?
Dunkie Yes! Truly truly true —just a bit of reading.
Lottie Ah-hah!
Dunkie And some spelling and some sums. But not much.
Lottie All right. What first? You choose.
Dunkie Reading.
Lottie Go on, then. Get your book.

Dunkie delves into his bag

Cross-fade to Christine and Fred

Fred (*more thoughtfully*) Did you check with their schools?
Christine Of course.
Fred Didn't they notice anything?
Christine Not according to the Head Teachers. Glowing reports!
    Both kids exemplary. Always immaculate; well behaved. Wish
    all kids were like that.
Fred But didn't they wonder about the parents?
Christine Well, they knew about the mother, of course. It happened
    almost as soon as they came here. After that — well — perhaps
    it seemed reasonable: lone parent with a business to run, all that.
    There was no reason to suspect anything.
Fred But — I mean they're kids, Christine. And it was months.
    How could they just keep going with nobody knowing?
Christine It was her. (*Indicating the diary*) Anything she couldn't
    do, she just asked.

Cross-fade to Mrs Reid, Lottie's teacher

Mrs Reid is sitting at her desk, marking some exercise books

Lottie approaches Mrs Reid, carrying the diary

Lottie Mrs Reid?

Mrs Reid Yes, Lottie?

Lottie May I ask you a question?

Mrs Reid Of course.

Lottie How do you make a shepherd's pie?

Mrs Reid A shepherd's pie?

Lottie Yes.

Mrs Reid Why do you want to know that?

Lottie Well, I really love the Home Ec. classes ...

Mrs Reid I know you do. You're very good at it, too.

Lottie Yes, but the recipes that we cook, they're always little things like biscuits or scones. I wondered how you made something bigger. You know, like a whole meal.

Mrs Reid Well, a whole meal is a bit ambitious, you know. Scones and biscuits might be easy recipes for you, Lottie. But, there are others in the class who find them quite hard. (*She grins*) Some of their scones turn out pretty hard, too. (*She chuckles*)

Lottie doesn't join in with her

Mrs Reid looks kindly at the serious-faced girl

Let's learn to walk before we try to run, eh?

Lottie Yes, Mrs Reid. It's just that ——

Mrs Reid Yes?

Lottie Nothing. just — my Dad ——

Mrs Reid (*realizing*) Oh, Lottie, of course, I'm sorry. I'd forgotten. There's just you and your dad at home, isn't there?

Lottie And Dunkie.

Mrs Reid Your brother. He's in the primary school isn't he?

Lottie Yes, P3.

Mrs Reid Of course. Do you get a lot of the housework to do?

Lottie Yes.

Mrs Reid It must be hard.

Lottie No, no. I like it. I'd like to do more, only there's a lot of things I don't know how.

Mrs Reid Don't you ask your Dad?

Lottie He's very busy working. He knows I can cope.

Mrs Reid I bet you can. (*She thinks for a moment, then pushes away the exercise books*) These can wait. Right. Shepherd's pie. Well, it's basically mashed potato and mince, of course. But I always like it with some carrots cooked in the mince.

Lottie Can I write it down?

Mrs Reid Of course.

Lottie opens her diary and makes notes

First, you peel some potatoes...

Cross-fade to Dunkie's bedroom

Dunkie is playing in his bedroom

Lottie enters

Lottie Teatime, Dunkie.

Dunkie What are we having?

Lottie Shepherd's pie.

Dunkie Awww! Again?

Lottie That was a real big one I made yesterday. There's still half of it left. C'mon, Dunkie, we can't afford to waste food. It costs a lot.

Dunkie Can we go and get an ice-cream afterwards, then?

Lottie All right, we'll go down to the paper shop. But only if you clean your plate — and that means the broccoli stalks, too!

Lottie and Dunkie exit

Cross–fade to Christine and Fred

Christine It's all here. Everything they ate; all the food groups ticked off to keep a balance.

Fred A regular little Mrs Beeton.

Christine Don't joke, Fred! Don't you dare. If this had been — Bosnia, or something — they'd have given this kid a medal.

Fred Lots of kids do extraordinary things.

Christine But look at the length of time she kept going, all on her own. She could have given up on day one, but she didn't. And where's it going to get her?

Fred Might turn out all right. Maybe the father will turn up.

Christine Perhaps.

Fred When did she first realize he was gone?

Christine (*leafing through the diary*) I don't know. I think she suspected quite quickly — maybe that's what prompted her to start keeping this diary. (*She finds a passage*) Here. This is a month or so into it. (*She hands Fred the book, pointing at the page*) This bit about bedtime.

Cross-fade to Dunkie's bedroom

Lottie is opening some envelopes, containing household bills. She writes the amounts in her exercise book. She pauses, and scrutinises one of the bills

Lottie (*to herself*) Why do we still get a phone bill even when we haven't telephoned anybody?

Dunkie enters

Lottie scrambles the papers away and then smiles at Dunkie

Bedtime, Dunkie.

Dunkie No, not yet.

Lottie Yes. It's school tomorrow.

Dunkie OK. (*Indicating the bills, hoping to change the subject*) What are those?

Lottie Sums.

Dunkie Is that your homework?

Lottie Sort of. C'mon, Dunkie — get ready for bed.

Dunkie pauses, then looks up at her solemnly

Dunkie Can we talk to Mummy please, Lottie?

Lottie You feeling lonely?

Dunkie nods

Course we can. You want to do it right now?
Dunkie Yes.

Lottie and Dunkie kneel down facing each other.Their heads bowed, their eyes closed and their hands clasped together in prayer

Lottie "Our Father ——"
Dunkie No! Our *Mother!*

Lottie briefly opens her eyes to look at Dunkie, then returns to her prayer

Lottie Our Mother, which art in heaven ... (*She takes a breath*) we're feeling a bit lonely, Mum. Particularly Dunkie. He misses you so much. I'm doing my best, but I miss you too, sometimes — quite a lot of times.
Dunkie (*whispering*) I've been good.
Lottie What?
Dunkie Tell her I've been good.
Lottie Tell her yourself.
Dunkie I've been a good boy, Mum. I tidy my room — a bit —and I don't ask for sweets every day. (*Gathering speed*) I swam a breadth in swimming on Tuesday and Mr Carter said, "Good lad", and I'm going to be a mushroom in the Easter show and ... (*He runs out of steam*) I wish you weren't dead.
Lottie We both wish you were still here, Mum (*she opens her eyes and delivers this to Dunkie as reassurance*) but we know that you still love us very much and we know that you will tell Jesus all about me and Dunkie so that He will keep a special eye on us. You mustn't worry about us and Dunkie mustn't worry either because he's got me. And even though he doesn't remember you very well — and I told him that's all right 'cos he was only little and can't be expected to. I do remember you and I remember all the things

you used to say. So it's really like you're still here — sort of. (*Speaking from her own heart*) I get most of it right, Mum. I give in a bit on Coca Cola but we don't eat a lot of sweets and I'm very good on E-numbers, just like you were. So we'll keep going and one day we know we'll all be together again. It's just a long time to wait. (*She thinks, but there's nothing left to say*) Get Jesus to send me one of your extra-special kisses and I'll pass it on to Dunkie when he's tucked up. 'Night, Mum.

Dunkie 'Night 'night, Mummy.

Lottie Thank you, Jesus. Amen.

Dunkie and Lottie open their eyes and look at each other for a moment

Right. Bed. I'll tuck you in, in a minute.

Dunkie Milk and juice?

Lottie OK. But do you think you could get it yourself, for once?

Dunkie exits

Lottie picks up the bills, but drops them again almost immediately. She rises and crosses to Dad's armchair. She sits down and curls up in a ball

Mum, if you're still there, could you ask Jesus to send Dad back to us? I told Dunkie he was away working but it's been five weeks now. I don't think he's going to come back on his own. He missed you so much, Mum, even more than us. I wanted to look after him, but he wouldn't let me. I did try, honestly. Sometimes I wonder if he might have gone to be with you and Jesus in heaven. I hope so, because I know that would make him happy. But if not — if he would come back — I would try to make him happy again. I know I could — I can do it — I can cope — (*Tearfully*) Oh, Mum —Mummy ... (*She trails off and buries her face in the in a corner of the chair in quiet, private tears*)

Cross-fade to Christine and Fred

Fred I still find it hard to believe they just got on with their lives, week after week, and nobody suspected anything.

Christine Why?

Fred It's just — well, these days you'd expect somebody to notice.

Christine Again — why? The only unusual thing is that these kids really were home alone. Most families have relatives or friends or — well, just people in contact: this family didn't, that's all. So with nobody to turn to, the two kids just got on with it.

Fred You'd still think ——

Christine Look, I bet if something had gone wrong, like they'd starved to death or something, there'd be hundreds of people who would say, "Well, I often saw her doing the shopping on her own and I used to wonder." That's the way it is, these days. We see appalling things every day. But it's none of our business.

Fred Well, it's our business now. (*He pauses and then leafs through the diary*) What did they do for money?

Christine Hole in the wall. She had the card and the PIN number.

Fred But the bills?

Christine Lots of standing orders at the bank. The rest she paid in cash. (*Indicating the diary*) All written down. Every penny accounted for. (*She thinks*) Can I ask you something?

Fred Go on.

Christine What's the balance of your bank account?

Fred You mean my overdraft?

Christine Whatever. How much?

Fred I'm not exactly sure.

Christine She was. And all the rest. Shopping lists, laundry schedules, the date her brother's school raincoat is next due for dry-cleaning ——

Fred All right, so she was organized. But it was still a hell of a risky situation. I mean, anything could have happened to them.

Christine Like what? What might have happened to them that couldn't have happened to any two kids, even with Mum and Dad sitting safely at home?

Fred Well, I mean, they might have had an accident; scalded themselves in the kitchen, or something.

Christine seizes the book and searches for a page. She finds it and reads

Christine "I'm not going to use the chip pan because I know it is dangerous and anyway Mum always said boiled potatoes were better for us."

Fred What if they fell ill?

Christine (*reading other passages*) "Dunkie sore throat this morning. Book appointment at doctor's"— "Dentist check-up after school" — Fred, this girl had it all sorted.

Fred Little Miss Perfect.

Christine (*frowning*) Yes. Too perfect, maybe. (*Thoughtfully*) I wonder. Perhaps she didn't write down absolutely everything.

Cross-fade to Dunkie's bedroom

Lottie, grim-faced, is pointing at Dunkie's scattered toys

Lottie Tidy it up!

Dunkie (*stubbornly*) Why?

Lottie Because it's a tip, Dunkie. I clear up every day and you just throw everything around again.

Dunkie They're my things. I can throw them around if I want to.

Lottie But we've got to be tidy, Dunkie.

Dunkie Why? Dad's not here to tell us off.

Lottie *I'm* here to tell you off, though.

Dunkie No, you're not. You're not the boss of me.

Lottie Well, somebody has to be the boss around here to get things done.

Dunkie Well, I should be the boss, not you.

Lottie Why?

Dunkie 'Cos I'm the boy. You're just a girl.

Lottie looks hurt

Lottie (*angrily*) What? You little ... (*She grabs his arm*)
Dunkie (*struggling to free himself*) Let go! Get off me!

Lottie (*more angrily*) Say you're sorry!
Dunkie No! Won't!
Lottie It's not fair! Say sorry!
Dunkie No. You're a bully. I hate you.
Lottie What?
Dunkie I hate you!

Lottie lashes out at Dunkie and smacks his head

Dunkie grasps hold of his head where Lottie hits him. He is stunned and shocked into silence by the blow

Lottie is equally stunned and appalled at what she has done

Dunkie (*looking up at Lottie, with tears welling in his eyes but with steel in his voice*) I wish you'd go away, too!

Dunkie runs off stage

Lottie makes to move after him

Lottie Dunkie ...

Dunkie has already gone

Lottie turns away, biting her lip. Suddenly she looks up in fury. Her hands are clenched into tight fists

Oh! Mum!! Why did you die?

Cross-fade to Christine and Fred

Fred What are you getting at?
Christine There must have been tensions. They wouldn't be human, otherwise.
Fred There probably were. But it's different with kids. They blow

hot and cold. They can be at each other's throats one second and
bosom pals the next. They don't have any — resentment.

Christine Fred, she's twelve. She loses her mother, her father walks
out and you're telling me that she doesn't resent it?

Fred Not necessarily. Not in any — damaging sense.

Christine No. There will be something there. She might not show
it. Might not even feel it, but it will be there. Deep inside. There
has to be.

Fred Why?

Christine Wouldn't you be screwed up if you were her?

Fred Maybe, but I'm not her. Come on, Chris. Don't make a
mountain out of a molehill.

Christine What did you say?

Fred I just mean that if it isn't obviously broken, let's not try to fix
it.

Christine What the hell do you mean, "mountain out of a
molehill"?

Fred I'm just saying I think you — maybe complicate things a bit
sometimes.

Christine That's what you think, is it?

Fred (*with tension*) Not just me ——

Christine Oh, that's what everybody thinks of me!

Fred No, I didn't mean that ...

Christine Then what did you mean, Fred?

Fred Look, it's not a criticism. It's great that you're enthusiastic.
And you have the energy and the skills to dig a bit deeper. We all
respect that, but ——

Christine But what?

Fred Oh, look, Christine, I don't want to get into all this.

Christine No, come on. You say you respect me, so have enough
respect to tell me the truth

Fred Well, you tend to get a bit — evangelistic.

Christine Evangelistic?

Fred Yes. (*Calmer*) You've got the makings of a damn good social
worker but you need to get a few more cases under your belt so
that you know which ones you need to get creative about and
which ones are quite simple.

Christine People's problems are never that simple.

Fred No, but sometimes the solution can be. Like this one. I mean, we've been chatting about these kids because the circumstances are interesting, but we both know what we're going to do about them.

Christine Do we?

Fred Of course we do.

Christine (*pointedly*) No, I don't, Fred. I haven't got your years of practical experience, so I can't arrive at instant conclusions like you. I'm still at the stage where I believe I have to weigh up all the possibilities.

Fred (*with restraint*) All I'm saying is that sometimes there aren't that many possibilities. Oh, come on, Chris, the last thing I want is a fight. Let's get them on their way and then I'll buy you a big drink.

Christine On their way where?

Fred To a foster home. It's not as if they're on drugs or been chucking bricks through windows. A pair of well-mannered, middle-class kids? Anyone would take them in.

Christine And that's it, is it?

Fred Well, can you think of a better alternative?

Christine Yes. I can. That's if you wouldn't think it was too — complicated.

Cross-fade to Dunkie's bedroom

Dunkie is alone in his room. He takes the majority of his toys and clothes, and scrapes them together in a heaped bundle to one side

Lottie enters carrying Dunkie's schoolbag

Dunkie I tidied my room!

Lottie So you did. Good boy. See, Dunkie, this is our home. We've got to keep it nice for when Daddy comes back. If we don't look after it, he might not come back and then we'll never be a family again. That's why it's important not to give up. (*She pauses to look at him*)

Dunkie (*hanging his head*) Sorry I shouted at you last night, Lottie.
Lottie I'm sorry too, Dunkie. Sorry I hit you.
Dunkie It's all right. It didn't hurt.
Lottie I didn't mean it to. (*Pause*) So you don't want me to go away, then?
Dunkie No.
Lottie And you don't hate me?

Dunkie shakes his head

Still want me as your BigSis?

Dunkie grins

And you're still my Little Bro. Come on. Time for school.

Lottie hands Dunkie the school bag

Dunkie Have you put my dinner money in?
Lottie No, I made you some sandwiches instead.
Dunkie Awww!
Lottie I thought it would be a change …
Dunkie I don't want a change. I like going to caff!
Lottie But the cafeteria's expensive, Dunkie. We have to look after our money as well as our bedrooms. OK?
Dunkie OK.
Lottie Tell you what. Next time we go shopping, you can pick your very favourite thing to have in your sandwiches. Deal?

Dunkie nods

Cross-fade to Mrs Reid

Lottie enters and approaches Mrs Reid

Lottie You wanted to see me, Mrs Reid?
Mrs Reid Yes, Lottie, Thanks for coming in during your break. (*She looks up at Lottie*)

Lottie (*nervously*) What is it, Mrs Reid?

Mrs Reid Nothing, really. It's just — you used to pop in to see me quite often, but not lately. I just wondered if anything was wrong.

Lottie No.

Mrs Reid You haven't got bored with Home Economics, have you?

Lottie No.

Mrs Reid Well, what then?

Lottie It's just — I was afraid I was asking you too many questions.

Mrs Reid But teachers love children to ask questions. It's what we're for.

Lottie I'm sorry.

Mrs Reid There's nothing to be sorry for. (*Pause*) I enjoyed our little chats at lunchtime. I felt I'd got to know you really well. (*Pause*) Well enough to notice when you started to change a bit.

Lottie Change?

Mrs Reid Yes. Oh, nothing much, just — not your usual sunny self, that's all. I've talked to the other teachers and you don't seem to be having problems with any of your subjects, so it must be something else. (*Pause*) Is it?

Lottie Is it what?

Mrs Reid Is it something else that's bothering you?

Lottie Nothing's bothering me.

Mrs Reid (*watching Lottie closely*) Things all right at home?

Lottie (*speaking quickly*) Yes. (*Collecting herself*) Everything's fine.

Mrs Reid Really?

Lottie Yes.

Mrs Reid You would tell me the truth, wouldn't you, Lottie?

Lottie (*firmly*) I never tell lies, Mrs Reid.

Mrs Reid Never?

Lottie Mum used to say that if you told a lie you'd never go to heaven. Before she died I was just scared of going to hell. But now I'd never tell a lie because if I didn't go to heaven I'd never see my mum again.

Mrs Reid Of course. You must miss her very much.

Lottie nods, biting back her tears

And your dad.

Lottie (*defensively*) Why should I miss my dad?

Mrs Reid No, I meant that he must miss your mum, too.

Lottie Oh. Yes.

Mrs Reid Does he talk to you about her?

Lottie No. I mean, he used to, but he hasn't mentioned her at all for months now.

Mrs Reid I see. Do you and he get on well?

Lottie How do you mean?

Mrs Reid Does he — get annoyed with you, or anything?

Lottie No. Not at all.

Mrs Reid Does he smack you when you do something naughty?

Lottie Never.

Mrs Reid (*carefully*) What about cuddles? Does he give you lots of hugs?

Lottie Mrs Reid, why are you asking all these questions about my dad?

Mrs Reid No reason, Lottie. Perhaps because I don't know him at all. I think he's the only parent I haven't met. I don't even see him at the school gate.

Lottie Perhaps you've just never noticed him.

Mrs Reid Perhaps.

Lottie I mean, since you've never met him, you wouldn't recognize him anyway, would you?

Mrs Reid I suppose not.

There is a long tense silence

Lottie May I go, Mrs Reid? I've got Maths.

Mrs Reid looks at Lottie for a moment, then relaxes for lack of another thread to follow

Mrs Reid All right.

Lottie exits

Cross-fade to Christine and Fred

Christine All I'm asking is why we shouldn't even consider it?

Fred Putting carers in to look after them in their own home? Have you any idea what that might cost?

Christine I'm looking at the possible cost of putting them in a foster home.

Fred Don't be daft, Chris. Twenty-four hour attendance, paying the mortgage, all the bills? Fostering's got to be cheaper.

Christine I'm not talking about money. I'm talking about the cost to *her*. She's struggled every day for months to keep that home going all by herself. And did a pretty good job, too. And now we expect her to walk calmly away from it and let somebody else run her life for her? You can't tell me that's not going to give her some problems.

Fred You can't be sure of that. Maybe she'll heave a huge sigh of relief and be glad to go back to being a kid.

Christine Oh, she might go back, all right. Go backward. You've seen it often enough. Kids from the best homes, well brought up. Something goes wrong, they're taken into care; some of them just go to pieces. Maybe they start to identify with other kids with problems or maybe it's a reaction to whatever happened to them, but it seems to hit them even harder than the really disadvantaged kids and they end up in a complete mess.

Fred Not always.

Christine It happens though. And is that the best we can do? Just chuck them into the system and trust to luck that they land on their feet? (*Pause*) Come on, Fred. They're an ideal case for in-home care.

Fred How do you make that out?

Christine Look, if she was an adult with learning difficulties and she'd been looking after a sick parent who died, we wouldn't dream of dragging her out of her own home.

Fred This isn't the same, Chris.

Christine Why not? She's proved that she can run the place with just a little bit of support. They could stay at the same school, keep the same doctor ... Christ, Fred, haven't they lost enough without us taking all the rest away from them?

Fred Christine, ordinarily I might agree with you, but under the circumstances—

Christine What circumstances?

Fred Well, you know what the budget's like.

Christine I don't give a damn what the budget's like. The budget's only there so that we can do the best we can for people!

Fred Exactly. For people. Not just this one case. It's not as if we didn't have other kids on our hands. And not with the advantages these two have had.

Christine What do you mean, advantages?

Fred Well, they've had a pretty good lifestyle up to now. That must have given them some skills and resources to help them cope. Lots of kids have nothing from day one.

Christine So we discriminate against them because they're middle-class?

Fred Not discrimination, just common sense! Making resources go as far as possible. We could fund basic care for these two and half a dozen others for the cost of in-home support. How can we justify giving this case special treatment?

Christine Because they're special kids?

Fred All kids are special.

Christine If they're all special, then none of them are special, are they, Fred? (*Pause*) So, if I made a recommendation for in-home care, you wouldn't support it?

Fred No.

Christine You wouldn't agree with any extra resources for them?

Fred Not while there's kids failing to get even minimum care, no.

Christine Nothing?

Fred I've nothing against them, Christine, but the way things are, I wouldn't spend a single extra pound on those two.

Christine And that's why she never wanted this day to come. (*She leafs through the diary*) LittleBro Morning and BigSis Afternoon.

Fred What?

Christine That's what she called today. The last morning when she could make sure that Dunkie was really happy. And then the afternoon when she would finally have to come to terms with reality.

Cross-fade to Mr Grant, the Bank Manager

Mr Grant is sitting in his chair

The clerk enters, carrying a piece of paper, and approaches Mr Grant

Clerk Excuse me, Mr Grant. May I have a word?

Grant Of course. What is it?

Clerk It's this account. I've been monitoring it for a while and it's rather peculiar.

Grant Really? In what way?

Clerk Well, you see ——

Grant What kind of account is it anyway?

Clerk Just a personal chequing account ——

Grant Opened recently?

Clerk No, about two years ago. With a balance transferred from one of our Southern branches.

Grant I see. Well, go on. What's so peculiar about it?

Clerk The point is ——

Grant Is it overdrawn?

Clerk No.

Grant Then what on earth's the problem?

Clerk I'm trying to tell you.

Grant Come on, spit it out. I've got a lot to do this afternoon.

Clerk As I was saying, there was an opening balance transferred from another account and then shortly afterwards a bigger lump-sum deposit. There's a note on the file that it was a life insurance claim. Fifty thousand. It seems the account holder's wife died.

Grant What's he do for a living?

Clerk Self - employed consultant of some sort. Operates as a sole trader. Except that he doesn't seem to trade very much. There were one or two deposits after the insurance money, but nothing substantial. Quite a few standing orders and direct debits — mostly for household and domestic items. A steady stream of cheques presented over the first year, together with some debit card items …

Grant Doesn't sound all that peculiar to me.

Clerk No, it's recently — over the last four months or so. Suddenly there's no more cheques presented and no more debit card charges.

Grant None?

Clerk None at all. Nothing but the standing orders and withdrawals from cash machines, mostly from the same machine.

Grant Let me see. (*He takes the paper and scans it*) Unusual, but hardly peculiar.

Clerk Suddenly doing all of his business in cash?

Grant Perhaps he prefers it. I'm old enough to remember a time when most people would rather deal in real money than bits of plastic. (*He looks up*) I know, I'm a dinosaur. I should be gung-ho about all this digicash and smart card nonsense, but I'm not. Sometimes I feel more like a computer programmer than a bank manager. Good job I'm retiring soon.

There is a hiatus, eventually broken by the clerk

Clerk What do you want to do?

Grant Well, I've always had a hankering to take up bowls ——

Clerk No, I mean about this account.

Grant Well, if it's not overdrawn, why do we need to do anything about it? Doesn't concern us.

Clerk It might concern us soon, though. If you add up the standing orders and compare it with the general rate of withdrawals, I calculate that the balance may not be enough to meet next month's commitments.

Grant I see. That's different.

Clerk Do you want me to put a stop on the account?

Grant Oh, no. No need for that. There's probably a simple explanation. An oversight or something. There may be another account somewhere. I've seen it happen before.

Clerk So we do nothing, then?

Grant Well, you could drop him a line drawing his attention to the situation.

Clerk Perhaps I should ring him up. Speak to him personally.

Grant Not at all. Just a nice letter. I'm sure that'll do the trick. Is that all you wanted?

Clerk Yes.
Grant Off you go, then.

Cross-fade to Dunkie's bedroom

*It is Dunkie's and Lottie's "special" morning and they are finishing
a game of bingo. They are dressed in their smart school clothes*

Dunkie (*without enthusiasm*) Bingo. I win.
Lottie Want to play again?
Dunkie No.
Lottie A different game?
Dunkie No thanks. Is my special morning finished yet?
Lottie (*looking at her watch*) No, there's a bit of time left. Why?
Dunkie I hoped that Daddy might be here for my special morning.
Lottie Did you?
Dunkie I thought he might come back. But I knew he wouldn't.
Lottie Why?
Dunkie (*sadly*) Because I didn't keep my bedroom nice.

Lottie seizes Dunkie's hand

Lottie Oh, Dunkie, that's not true. You did. You kept it really nice.
    It's not your fault that Dad went away. Just like Mummy dying.
    It's just an accident. Not anybody's fault. (*She hugs Dunkie*) Oh,
    I didn't want you to feel sad. Not on your special morning.
Dunkie Lottie, why is it only a morning?
Lottie Don't you remember, we talked about it. We shared the day
    in half. You could do what you wanted in the first half and then
    I had things to do in the second half. LittleBro morning and BigSis
    afternoon.
Dunkie What are you going to do in BigSis afternoon?
Lottie Oh, we don't want to talk about that yet. This is still your half.
Dunkie I don't want any more of my half. (*He looks at Lottie*) Tell
    me.
Lottie You really want to know?

Dunkie nods, solemnly

(*Pulling the brown envelope out of her diary*) It's this.

Dunkie I didn't see the postman this morning.

Lottie I've had it for a few days.

Dunkie What is it?

Lottie It's for Daddy, but I opened it. It's from the bank. We haven't any money left.

Dunkie But we have got money. We sold the television.

Lottie Try to understand, Dunkie. With Daddy being away, he hasn't been paying money into the bank. There was some to start with, but we've been using it up. I thought that if we sold some things like the television we could get money that way. But the man in that shop didn't give us much. Anyway he was suspicious, so I didn't want to go back. I've been trying to make the money last out.

Dunkie I know. No more comics!

Lottie I drew comics for you myself.

Dunkie I know, but it's not the same.

Lottie No, you're right. It isn't. And that's why we can't go on.

Dunkie What do you mean?

Lottie We can't go on doing things for ourselves. Not without money. We're going to have to go and tell somebody —about us. About Mummy and Daddy and —everything. We need help.

Dunkie No we don't, Lottie. You can do everything. Shepherd's pie and ironing and ——

Lottie It's money, Dunkie. You need money for everything.

Dunkie You can have my pocket money.

Lottie I give you your pocket money in the first place.

Dunkie It's my birthday soon. I'll ask for money instead of presents.

Lottie There's only me to give you presents. We don't know anybody else! That's the point, Dunkie. If our grannies and grandads had been still alive, if we had any aunties or uncles, we could go to them. But we don't. We don't even know anybody in this new place. It's always just been you and me, and Mummy and Daddy. And now it's just you and me. (*She tenderly brushes a cowlick of hair away from Dunkie's eyes*)

Dunkie I know! Let's win the Lottery!

Lottie Oh, Dunkie…

Dunkie Come on. We can pick the numbers from the Bingo.

Lottie It's a waste of time.

Dunkie Please, Lottie. You said I could choose what to do. There's still a bit of my special morning left.

Lottie (*getting her diary*) All right. I'll draw you a lottery ticket.

Dunkie Can't we have a real one?

Lottie They cost a whole pound.

Dunkie Haven't we got a pound?

Lottie It doesn't make any difference, Dunkie. Even if we had the money, I couldn't buy a real ticket. They won't sell them to kids.

Dunkie Draw one, then. You're a good drawer, Lottie. I bet it looks as real as real!

Lottie All right, then. Go on, then. You pick six numbers.

Dunkie (*selecting counters off the Bingo board*) Twenty two — eighteen — sixty five ——

Lottie No, that's too big. They have to be smaller.

Dunkie OK. Forty three — thirty two — (*he smiles*) and twelve for your age and seven for mine.

Lottie (*completing her writing and showing Dunkie*) Right. There you are. Cross your fingers and make a wish.

Dunkie Will we be lucky?

Lottie I wish I knew, Dunkie. (*Pause*) Do you want to do something else?

Dunkie No.

Lottie Is LittleBro morning finished?

Dunkie nods

Let's get ready, then.

Lottie rises and gets a smart raincoat out of a cupboard. She brushes a stray speck of dust off the coat and dresses Dunkie over the following lines

Dunkie Where are we going?

Lottie There'll be an office somewhere with people who know what to do.

Dunkie Where is it?

Lottie I don't know.

Dunkie So how will we find it?
Lottie We'll ask at the police station.
Dunkie Police station! They'll lock us up!
Lottie Maybe. But not in prison.
Dunkie What do you mean?

Lottie pauses and looks at him very seriously

Lottie Dunkie, BigSis afternoon is going to be a bit different from
LittleBro morning. We're going to have to live somewhere else,
maybe with another mummy and daddy. (*Pause*) I don't even
know if they'll keep us together.
Dunkie I don't want another mummy and daddy.
Lottie Neither do I. But people will say that we need them. They're
not going to listen to what we want, Dunkie. They're not being
nasty, it's just that they're grown ups and they think that they
know what's best for kids. They'll think they're being kind.
Dunkie I don't want to be away from you, Lottie.
Lottie And I don't want to be away from you. Maybe it won't
happen. But things we don't want, do happen sometimes. We
didn't want to be away from Mummy, did we?

Dunkie shakes his head

And Daddy didn't want to be away from us either — not really.
He just got lost in being sad. (*She finishes buttoning up his coat*)
And it's only for a little while anyway. We'll be back together
again soon.
Dunkie You mean when we're with Jesus?
Lottie No. Much sooner than that. Just a few years. When I'm
eighteen. Maybe before that. When they'll let me do things for
myself, wherever you are, I'll come and get you and then I'll look
after you again.
Dunkie Lottie — when you come for me — can that be another
LittleBro morning?
Lottie No, Dunkie, not a morning. I'm going to make it a LittleBro
rest of your life!

Lottie and Dunkie stand facing each other, holding hands

A slow cross-fade to Christine and Fred

Christine is putting down the telephone

Fred At least they'll be together. That's a good place.
Christine And we'll keep trying to find the father. You never know.
Fred Sounds like he has his own problems, though.
Christine Yes. Might even be better off without him.

A pause

Fred They'll be all right. Those are really nice people. I've known
the lady for years. She'll look after them like a mother hen.
Christine She'll have to — (*she throws down the diary*) she's got
a hard act to follow!

Lottie's pretend Lottery ticket flutters out from the diary

Fred What's that?

Christine picks it up

Christine It's a Lottery ticket. Not a real one, she's drawn it. For
her brother, probably.

Christine and Fred look at each other

Fred reaches out and takes the ticket. He fingers it, thoughtfully

Fred Isn't the mid-week draw tonight?
Christine What?

Fred waves the ticket

You mean ... ? "I wouldn't spend a single extra pound on them",
that's what you said.

Fred looks at her

Oh, Fred, don't be ridiculous. Life's not like that.

Fred takes a pound coin out of his pocket and holds it up beside the ticket

Christine looks at Fred directly but sympathetically

    Who's romanticizing now?
Fred (*deflated slightly*) Yeah. You're right, of course.
Christine Anyway, I'm not sure it isn't too late. I think the tills close in a few minutes.
Fred Absolutely. Silly idea. (*He tosses the ticket into the waste bin and puts the coin back in his pocket*)
Christine (*warmly*) Nice thought though. (*She picks up a shoulder bag and puts it over her shoulder*) I'm going to call it a day. You coming for that drink?
Fred (*indicating the fat file he was reading at the beginning*) I'll just finish this, I think.
Christine Right. See you tomorrow, Fred.

    Christine exits

Fred opens his file and reads for a moment. He pauses, sets the file aside and roots in the waste bin. Eventually, he finds the lottery ticket. He fishes out the coin from his pocket once again

Fred All right. Maybe a single extra pound.

    Fred exits

A slow cross-fade to Dunkie's bedroom

Dunkie and Lottie are standing holding hands. If adults played them in the main scenes, this is where the real children take over the roles once more. They are dressed exactly as we last saw the adult actors: in smart outdoor school clothes

Lottie picks up a small suitcase

Dunkie picks up his school bag and looks around anxiously, searching for something

Lottie steps forward and retrieves his loved-to-bits teddy-bear from the bedroom jumble. She holds it out to Dunkie

Dunkie clasps the teddy-bear close to himelf

Lottie takes Dunkie's hand and begins to lead him upstage out of the bedroom

Dunkie turns at the last moment and takes a last look round. His face is serious

Lottie pauses and watches the little boy

The light begins to fade into circles around the figures

The small figures exit quietly into the darkness still hand in hand

The light fades to black-out

FURNITURE AND PROPERTY LIST

<small>Lottie's and Dunkie's Bedroom</small>

On stage: Cupboard. *In it*: A raincoat
Bed. *On it*: A mound of bedding
Dad's armchair to the corner of the room
Chair. *On it*: A pile of neatly folded clothes and Dunkie's
         school clothes
Television
Teddy-bear
Scattered assortment of toys, books, and clothes

Off stage: Exercise book. *With it*: A brown envelope, torn open,
      between the pages. A ball point pen clipped to the book
      (**Lottie**)
Tray. *On it*: A plastic bowl filled with cereal, a matching cup
      of juice and a teacup with a single small flower in it
      (**Lottie**)
Television remote control (**Dad**)
Newspaper (**Lottie**)
School bag (**Dunkie**)
Some envelopes containing household bills (**Lottie**)
Bingo board game. *On it*: Some numbered counters
Small suitcase (**Lottie**)

Personal: **Dad**: Bank debit card

<small>Christine's and Fred's office</small>

On stage: Office desk. *On it*: A telephone, files and a jumble of paper
Two office chairs

Waste paper bin
Two manilla files. One thick with paper, the other new with
    a few papers
Shoulder bag(**Christine**)
Cheap exercise book, identical to Lottie's. *In it*: A pretend
    Lottery ticket

Personal: **Fred**: Pound coin

A School Classroom

On stage: Desk: *On it*. some exercise books
                  Chair

*During the black-out on page 25 the exercise books are struck for Mr
        Grant, the bank manager*

Off stage: An official looking piece of paper (**The Clerk**)

LIGHTING PLOT

Property fittings required: A television
Four acting areas

To open: **Dunkie's** *bedroom in semi-darkness*

Cue 9   **Christine**: "Every detail."   (Page 11)
             Cross-fade to **Dunkie's** *bedroom*

Cue 10   **Dunkie** delves into his bag   (Page 12)
             Cross-fade to **Christine's** *and* **Fred's** *office*

Cue 11   **Christine**: "... she just asked."   (Page 12)
             Cross-fade to **Mrs Reid**

Cue 12   **Mrs Reid**: "First, you peel some potatoes ..."   (Page 14)
             Cross-fade to **Dunkie's** *bedroom*

Cue 13   **Lottie** and **Dunkie** exit   (Page 14)
             Cross-fade to **Christine's** *and* **Fred's** *office*

Cue 14   **Christine**: "This bit about bedtime."   (Page 15)
             Cross-fade to **Dunkie's** *bedroom*

Cue 15   **Lottie** buries her face in **Dad's** armchair   (Page 17)
             Cross-fade to **Christine's** *and* **Fred's** *office*

Cue 16   **Chistine**: "...write down absolutely everything. "   (Page 19)
             Cross-fade to **Dunkie's** *bedroom*

Cue 17   **Lottie**: "Oh! Mum!! Why did you die?"   (Page 20)
             Cross-fade to **Christine's** *and* **Fred's** *office*

Cue 18   **Christine**: "...think it was too — complicated."   (Page 22)
             Cross-fade to **Dunkie's** *bedroom*

Cue 19   **Lottie**: " ...sandwiches. Deal?" **Dunkie** nods   (Page 23)
             Cross-fade to **Mrs Reid**

Cue 20   **Mrs Reid**: "All right." **Lottie** exits   (Page 25)
             Cross-fade to **Christine's** *and* **Fred's** *office*

Cue 21   **Christine**: " ...come to terms with reality."   (Page 27)
             Cross-fade to **Mr Grant**, *the bank manager*

EFFECTS PLOT

No Cues